Giovanna Magi

ISRAEL

**BEERSHEBA • BETHLEHEM • EILAT • HAIFA • HEBRON •
JAFFA • JERICHO • JERUSALEM • MASADA • NAZARETH • TEL AVIV •**

AKKO • ASHKELON • AVDAT • BANYAS • CAPERNAUM • CAESAREA •
DEAD SEA • DIMONA • EIN KAREM • GOLAN • KIBBUTZ AYELET HASHAHAR • MEGIDDO •
MOUNT TABOR • QUMRAN • SAFED • SODOM • TABGHA • TEL QASILA • TIBERIAS •

BONECHI & STEIMATZKY

*The Temple of Herod in the model of ▶
Jerusalem at the Holyland Hotel. The
model, built on a scale of 1:50,
depicts Jerusalem as it must have
appeared in 66 A. D., the end of the
Second Temple era, just before the
Romans destroyed the Temple in 70
A. D. The model's construction was
supervised by Prof. Michael Avi Yonah
and was based on descriptions of the
city given by Josephus Flavius, the
Talmud and Mishna.*

CONTENTS

© Copyright 1992 by CASA EDITRICE BONECHI, Via Cairoli 18/b, Florence - Italy — Telex 571323 CEB — Fax 055/5000766 —

All rights reserved. No part of this book may be reproduced without the written permission of the Publisher —
Printed in E.E.C. by Centro Stampa Editoriale Bonechi —
Translated by Claire Seminario —

The photos belong to the archives of BONECHI Publishing Group and were taken by Garo Nalbandian and
Alessandro Saragosa

ISBN 88-7009-258-5

JERUSALEM

Condensing Jerusalem's four-thousand-year history into a few pages is difficult indeed, particularly since Jerusalem's past is so immensely varied and dramatic.

Situated in the Judean mountains, Jerusalem is a city sacred to humanity. For Moslems, it is El Kuds, the Holy; for Jews, Yerushalim, their capital city since the time of King David; for Christians, the site of Christ's Passion and Crucifixion. The name «Jerusalem» means «City of Peace», but how few have been the periods of peace in its history! Jerusalem has been invaded and laid waste by the Egyptians, Babylonians, Greeks, Romans, Persians, Moslems, Christians, Mamelukes and the Turks.

Jerusalem's first inhabitants lived on the hill south of the Temple Mount area which Josephus called the Ophel. They were a Canaanite tribe called the Jebusites. Their city had been mentioned in an Egyptian Execration Text of the second millennium B.C. as «Ursalim», one of a long list of cities conquered by Pharaoh. In 1000 B.C., David conquered Jerusalem and bought the top of Mount Moriah from the Jebusite king Arauna on which to build an altar to the Lord. He transferred the Ark of the Covenant, symbolizing the union between God and his people, there from Hebron.

It had accompanied the People of Israel throughout the long years of wandering in the desert before arriving in the Promised Land and had gone with them into many battles.

Solomon, son of David and Bathsheba, also chose Mount Moriah as the site for the grand and sumptuous First Temple he built around 950 B.C. The Temple itself was later destroyed but the wisdom of its builder would be remembered for centuries to come. After Solomon's death, discord among the tribes split his kingdom into two parts: Israel in the north and Judah, with its capital in Jerusalem, in the south. The kingdom of Israel succumbed to Assyrian advances shortly thereafter and became an Assyrian province. Judah resisted a bit longer. While King Sennacherib failed to conquer Jerusalem in 701 B.C., the Babylonian Nebuchadnezzar succeeded to do so in 587 B.C. He sacked the city, destroyed the Temple and took thousands of Jews back with him to Babylonia. This Babylonian exile lasted nearly fifty years, until the Persian King Cyrus conquered Babylonia and allowed the exiles to begin their return to Judah. Approximately one hundred years later, Nehemiah the Prophet and Ezra the Scribe supervised the

3

Panorama of Jerusalem from the Mount of Olives. On the left, the site of the Temple with the Dome of the Rock.

rebuilding of the Temple in Jerusalem as well as the walls around the city, which were completed in record time. With the arrival of Alexander the Great in 333 B.C., the country saw the beginning of its «Hellenistic» era, when Greek pagan ideas infiltrated the Jewish culture and led to serious clashes. When Emperor Antiochus Epiphanes IV declared himself divine and commanded the Jews to sacrifice pigs on their altars to him, the Maccabbean Revolt ignited, culimating in the ousting of the Greeks (Seleucids) from Jerusalem in 164 B.C. For the next century, the Hasmonean dynasty of Jewish kings ruled the country. In 63 B.C. as Pompey led his legions into Jerusalem, the Land (now composed of Judah, Samaria, the Galilee, the Golan and the Negev) became part of the Roman Empire. In 37 B.C., the Roman Senate gave the title of king to Herod, who would later be known as Herod the Great. Despite the resentment the population felt toward him, Herod brought Jerusalem to unprecedented magnificence by expanding and rebuilding the Temple and by his many other monumental building projects in the city.

After his death in the year 4 B.C., his kingdom was divided among his three sons. During the reign of one of them, Herod Antipas, Jesus was crucified on orders of the Procurator, Pontius Pilate, in Jerusalem.

The ever more frequent and bloody Jewish rebellions against the heavy-handed Romans led to the destruction of Herod's Temple by Titus in the year 70 A.D. Sixty years later, another major revolt led by a Jew named Bar Kochba, precipitated the complete leveling of the city of Jerusalem by the Roman general Hadrian. On its ruins he erected the pagan city of Aelia Capitolina and forbade Jews to set foot there. At the same time, he changed the name of the country to «Palestina». Most of the Jews were forced to leave by famine, persecution and intolerably heavy taxes. Thus began the great Dispersion of the Jewish people throughout the world.

When the Roman Emperor Constantine embraced Christianity in the early fourth century, the Byzantine Era began. Jerusalem became a Christian city, with the Holy Sepulcher its centerpiece. The Persians, under Cosroe II, invaded the city, destroyed the Holy Sepulcher and deported much of the population in 614 A.D. Twenty-three years later, Omar led the Moslem invasion of Jerusalem. For the next four hundred years, Jerusalem took on the complexion of Islam, and was called by the Moslems, «El Kuds», «the Holy». According to the Koran, Abraham, David and Solomon were also great prophets before Mohammed. The tradition that Mohammed made his «Night Journey» to heaven was associated with the Temple Mount, where the Dome of the Rock and the Al-Aksa Mosque were built in 691 and 703 A.D., respectively.

In 1099, the Crusaders arrived from Europe to liberate

Christian holy sites from the «infidels». They conquered Jerusalem and immediately set about rebuilding their holiest shrine, the Holy Sepulcher. Jerusalem became a city of churches and monasteries until 1187, when the Moslem leader Saladin recaptured it. The city was to come into Christian hands once again before the Crusaders were summarily ousted from the country by the Mamelukes at the end of the thirteenth century. Jerusalem sank into a dusty, poverty-stricken stupor, its population dwindling to a mere 11,000 by mid-nineteenth century.

Following the Crimean War, interest in the Holy Land was rekindled. The first Jewish neighbourhoods began to crop up around the walled city in the 1860's, and by 1915, the Jewish population of the city had swelled to 100,000.

On December 9, 1917, the British General Allenby accepted the surrender of the city of Jerusalem from the Turks and three years later, the British Mandate of Palestine began. Finding the Jewish-Arab rivalry in Palestine too great a burden, England relinquished its Mandate in 1947. On November 29 of that year, the United Nations voted to partition the Mandate between the Jews and the Arabs of Palestine. Within hours the newborn Jewish state was attacked by its Arab neighbours on all sides, a conflict which was to become known as the Independence War of 1948. A year and a half later, ceasefire lines were drawn, placing Jerusalem's Old City with all its holy sites in Jordan and the newer, western side of the city in Israel. A wall was built through the heart of Jerusalem, cutting off the population of each side from the other for nineteen years.

On June 5, 1967, Jordanian artillery opened fire on the Jewish side of the city. It was a thoughtless act that within 48 hours brought about the reunification of the city under Jewish control. On June 27, the State of Israel annexed the Old City and tore down the wall which had divided east from west. It was as though a dam had burst; people flooded from each side of the city to the other, some seeing the opposite end for the first time ever. Amid tremendous excitement, intermingling and reunions took place. However, once inside the Old City, the Jews made the painful discovery that the Jordanians had blown up the twenty-seven synagogues and many of the religious schools there. Those which hadn't been destroyed had been used as latrines, stables and garbage heaps. But the Wall, the Wailing Wall, had survived the vandalism. Its environs were cleared and thousands of Jews poured into the Old City to touch and kiss its ancient stones for the first time in two thousand years. It now became known as the Western Wall because it would attract all people not just in sorrow, as in the past, but in joy as well. The long exile was over. Returned to their city, Jews rebuilt her synagogues and houses, lanes and public squares with loving tenderness. Throughout two thousand years of separation from Jerusalem, Jews have repeated each day, «Next Year in Jerusalem!» Today, their hopes of returning to Zion have been realized.

Menorah - The seven-branched candlelabrum («menorah») has been the symbol of the Jewish people since ancient times. This giant bronze menorah, on which there appear twenty-nine scenes from Jewish history sculpted in bas-relief, was done by Benno Elkan and presented as a gift from the British Parliament to the State of Israel in 1956. It is inscribed with the words: «The Menorah is a symbol of the light of faith and hope which has led the Jewish people for four thousand years often through martyrdom in their mission of upholding the religion of righteousness among men and between nations. It is the emblem of the State of Israel. This menorah commemorating the great personages and events of Jewish history is presented to the Knesset as a gift from Britain. 1956».

The windmill - In the mid-19th century, when conditions inside Jerusalem's Jewish quarter became unbearably crowded, philanthropists Sir Moses Montefiori and Yehuda Touro built new housing outside the city's walls. Jews who were courageous enough to venture outside what is now called «The Old City» were accommodated there. Montefiori built the windmill on the hill above this new housing complex for the residents to mill their own flour. It never functioned, however, because it was relatively too low on the landscape. Still, it is one of Jerusalem's most familiar landmarks.

Ramot - At the end of the Six Day War in 1967, the walls and barbed wire fences which had cut Jerusalem in half were taken down. The previously divided Jewish and Arab sections spilled into one another and the city was reunited. In the early 1970's, several new neighbourhoods were constructed around Jerusalem as a «security belt»: Ramot, Neveh Yaacov, Pisgat Zeev and Givat Zeev to the north, Talpiot Mizrach and Gilo to the southeast.

Jaffa Road - Named Jaffa Road because it begins at Jaffa Gate and leads the traveler in the direction of the port of Jaffa on the Mediterranean coast, this busy street in the heart of Jerusalem's shopping district is a must for every visitor.

The new neighbourhood of Ramot in northern Jerusalem. ▶

Early morning on Jaffa Road, one of Jerusalem's main ▶
streets.

The Menorah which stands outside Israel's parliament, the Knesset.

The windmill, one of Jerusalem's most familiar landmarks.

The Damascus Gate, with its festive animation.

From left to right and top to bottom: ▶
Herod's Gate, the Lion's Gate, the
Golden Gate and the Zion Gate.

The Walls and Gates - Jerusalem's Old City is surrounded by a splendid two and a half mile limestone wall built by the Turkish ruler, Suleiman the Magnificent, between 1536 and 1539. The walls have seven gates. The most beautiful is the **Damascus Gate**, with its many turrets. Recent excavations have revealed the ancient Roman entrance beneath it. **Herod's Gate** or the Flower Gate, leads the visitor into the Moslem Quarter of the city. Towards the Mount of Olives is the **Lions Gate**, called St. Stephen's Gate by the Christians who believe that the saint was martyred there. The Arabs call it Bab Sittia Maryan (The Virgin Mary's Gate) because her birthplace is thought to be inside this gate. The **Golden Gate**, or **Mercy Gate**, is divided into two arches which were blocked up by the Moslems. Tradition has it that Jesus passed through here on his way to the Temple. It is also believed that the gate was built by the Byzantines over foundations laid by King Solomon. The **Dung Gate**, named thus because the city's Christian inhabitants threw their garbage on the ruins of the Temple Mount in Byzantine times, leads the visitor directly into the Western Wall area. The **Zion Gate**, which gives access to the Jewish Quarter, is called by the Arabs Bab el Daoud (David) because it faces Mount Zion, the traditional burial place of King David. The **Jaffa Gate**, one of the city's busiest gates, stands at the beginning of Jaffa Road, leading west to the coast and port of Jaffa. Called Bab el Khalil in Arabic, the gate was opened and a road paved through it in 1898 to allow Kaiser Wilhelm's carriage to pass through. The **New Gate** was opened in 1889.

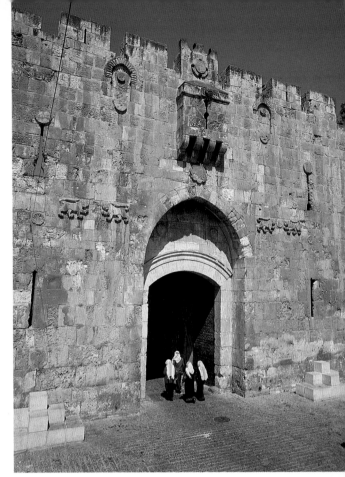

The Jaffa Gate.

The Tower of David, with its characteristic minarets.

The Citadel and Tower of David - Situated next to Jaffa Gate, the Citadel encompasses an area where once stood three towers built by King Herod: the Phasael Tower (named for his brother), Hippicus Tower (names for his friend) and the Miriamne Tower (named for his wife). They were to guard Herod's adjacent palace and were later spared destruction by Titus' Roman army in order to house his Twelfth Legion. During the Byzantine era, it was in such a state of ruin that philosophers and recluses chose it as a place of meditation. It was used as a fortress headquarters in the 12th century by the Crusaders, who repaired its walls and surrounded it by a moat. The Moslem Mamelukes demolished it in 1239 and it remained in a state of abandon until 1335 when the Turks repaired its walls and added the minaret known today as the **Tower of David**. The Citadel became a British base during the Mandate (1917-1948) and then a Jordanian one until 1967. Today, it houses several museums and is famous for the sound and light shows presented on its walls.

The suggestive spectacle of sound and light in the citadel.

Arch of the Hurva Synagogue and the
façade of the Tiferet Israel Synagogue.

◄ The reconstruction of the ancient north-south road.

◄ The Cardo: one aspect
of the recently restored Jewish quarter.

The Jewish Quarter - Devoid of Jews between the reign
of Emperor Hadrian and the end of the Crusades, the
Jewish Quarter was populated by rabbis and their
students between the 13th century and the 1948 Independence War. It was taken by the Jordanian Legion and
almost completely leveled by the time of the Six Day War
in 1967. Since then, the Jewish Quarter has been
undergoing careful archaeological examination and restoration, and its homes and streets have been rebuilt. The
Hurva Synagogue, blown up in 1948, had been built in
1740 on the remains of a 13th century synagogue and it is
recognizable by its single restored arch. The **Tiferet Israel
Synagogue**, its name meaning «glory of Israel», was one
of the last pockets of resistance before the quarter fell in
1948. It can be identified by its three arched en-
trances.

Wilson Arch - Located to the left of the Western (or Wailing) Wall, this arch was named for Charles Wilson who discovered it in 1865. Beneath this medieval structure lies the original Herodian arch which supported the bridge connecting Second Temple Jerusalem's Upper City with the Temple Mount. Ongoing excavations have revealed another seventeen courses of the beautifully dressed Herodian stone beneath the present floor level.

The Broad Wall - Discovered during excavations in the Jewish Quarter immediately after the Six Day War, this seven meter wide stone wall was part of the fortification King Hezekiah built to encompass his city in 701 B. C. Many refugees from the northern tribes of Israel had come to Jerusalem for protection from the Assyrians who threatened the north. They settled to the west and were included in the city when this wall was completed.

Herodian Quarter - Beneath the imposing Wohl Torah Study Center are the remains of several mansions dating from the Herodian Dynasty period (37 B. C.-70 A. D.). The lower floors preserved here are especially rich, with many colorful mosaics and frescoes, and are full of bath tubs, ritual bath pools (mikvehs) and cisterns. These mansions belonged to the aristocracy of the Second Temple Period, the Sadduccees, who were the priests and Temple administrators.

◄ *Jews in prayer at the Wilson Arch.*

◄ *View of the Wailing Wall.*

General view of the Wailing Wall dominated by the dome of the Omar mosque.

WESTERN (WAILING) WALL

Symbol of Jewish faith and object of Jewish pilgrimage from all over the world, the Western Wall (Hakotel Hama'aravi) is a remnant of the western retaining wall of Herod's Temple Mount. It acquired the name «Wailing Wall» because during the long exile of the Jewish people from the city, they could return only once a year to mourn the destruction of the Temple. Throughout nearly two thousand years of exile, Jews from all parts of the world turned their faces in prayer toward this Wall in the hope of return. The Wall became the symbol of reconquest of the

city and reunification of the Jewish State when, in June of 1967, the first Israeli soldiers reached it. It was an unforgettably emotional event in the history of the Jewish people. Today, there is always someone praying at the Western Wall, whether throngs of people gathered for the holidays or just a few lingerers in the middle of the night.

One well-known custom associated with the Wall is to insert small papers on which are written prayers into the fissures between the monumental Herodian stones.

Jewish tourists insert their prayers to God between the Wall's bricks.

Two moments of the Bar Mitzvah: this ceremony takes place when male children reach their thirteenth birthday. The great Sefer Torah in painted wood guards the book of laws.

The recent excavations under the site of the Temple. To the right, the silver dome of the Al Aqsa Mosque.

Dung Gate.

The Dung Gate - The Dung Gate, on the southern wall of Jerusalem's Old City, leads the visitor into the Western Wall Plaza. It received this name during the Byzantine era when the city's residents threw their garbage here in the area of the Temple Mount.

The Al-Aqsa-Mosque - The Al Aqsa Mosque can be identified by its black dome and its arched, Romanesque facade. Its name means «the farthest away», referring to the place farthest from Mecca and Medina that the Prophet would reach on his Night Journey. The modest mosque built by Walid in 709 was later greatly enlarged by the Templar Crusaders who entered the city in 1099. They named their new basilica «Templum Solomonis». With the ousting of the Crusaders from the country by the Mamelukes in the late 13th century, the entire structure became the Al Aqsa Mosque. It suffered considerable

◄ *Exterior and interior of the El Aqsa Mosque.*

On this and the following page, the crowd in the Mosque of Omar during the Ramadan.

damage due to earthquakes but underwent massive restoration between 1938 and 1943. During this time, the marble columns (a gift of Mussolini) and the ceiling (given by the then Egyptian king Farouk), were added. The mosque has witnessed two recent dramatic events. On July 20, 1951, Jordan's King Abdullah was assassinated at the door. Today's King Hussein, who was with him, was miraculously saved by the heavy decorations he was wearing on his chest. Traces of the flying bullets are still visible on a column there. The other event occurred in 1969 when a crazed Australian set a fire inside the mosque causing damage that is still being repaired today.

19

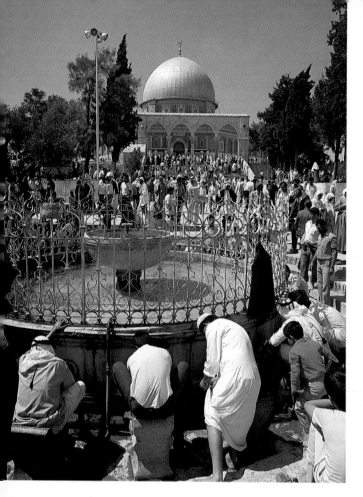

Detail of the sacred rock inside the ▶
Mosque of Omar.

THE TEMPLE SITE AND DOME OF THE ROCK

The gate through which one ascends the Temple Mount from the Western Wall area is called the Mughrabi Gate, recalling the North Africa Moslems whose homes once clustered nearby.

The Haram es Sharif, or «The Nobel Sanctuary», covers about thirty acres in the shape of a trapezoid. It is sacred to the Moslems as the third place of pilgrimage after Mecca and Medina. It is sacred to the Jews as the site where Abraham nearly sacrificed his son, Isaac. Here stood Solomon's Temple, of which no trace remains, but which was meticulously described in the Books of Ezekiel and Kings. The Temple, resplendent with its carved cedarwood panels and gold-plated rosettes, housed the Ark of the Covenant which held the Ten Commandments,

the «covenant» between God and the Jewish people. Only the High Priest could enter the Holy of Holies where the Ark was kept, and then only on the Day of Atonement (Yom Kippur). The Temple was destroyed by Nebuchadnezzar in 587 B. C. and the Ark was lost. What is visible today are actually remains of the Second Temple, built by Herod the Great around 20 B. C. Its enormous foundations were supported by four retaining walls and many internal arches known today as Solomon's Stables. When the Moslems arrived there in 638 A. D., they found the Temple Mount had been covered with refuse. They cleared it and reinstated it as a place of worship since, according to Moslem tradition, Mohammed made his ascent into heaven (Night Journey) from here. In 687

The so-called Stables of King Solomon:
here the Crusaders kept their horses and camels.

A.D., Ommayad caliph Abd el Malik decided to erect a mosque on the spot and entrusted the job to Christian-Byzantine architects. Perched on an embankment accessible by flights of steps on four sides, the splendid **Dome of the Rock** (sometimes called the **Mosque of Omar**) presides over the entire Temple Mount area. Octagonal in form, it consists of a high base of colored marble, a 16th century reconstruction of the original model, from which rises the round drum covered with arabesque tiles of azure blue majolica. This beautiful ceramic decoration is thanks to Suleiman the Magnificent, who in 1552, had the famous Persian factories of Kashan fire this majolica to replace the previous mosaic walls of the mosque. It is crowned by the gold-colored dome, which was originally lead. Inside, the prayers and praises of Allah visible on the frieze were done in 1876 by the famous Turkish calligrapher, Mohammed Chafik. The interior of the mosque, with its double rows of 12 pillars and 28 monolithic columns is illuminated by 36 stained-glass windows. A carved wood screen encircles the bare bedrock in the center. A few steps lead to the grotto beneath the rock known to the Moslems as the «cave of the spirits». It is believed that the souls of pious Moslems gather here on Thursday evenings just before the Moslem Sabbath, Friday.

The exterior of the Church of St. Anne and, next to it, the excavations where the pool of Bathsheba or Probatical Pool, with its two pools and five doorways, was found. Here, Jesus cured the paraplegic.

The church's crypt.

Church of St. Anne - A true gem of Crusader architecture, the church of St. Anne is one of Jerusalem's best preserved medieval structures. This church of austere, simple beauty, maintained by the White Fathers since 1878, was built in the place to which tradition assigns the birth of Mary. Her parents, Anne and Joachim, had their home here. It was built in 1142 at the request of Queen Arda, widow of Baldwin I of Jerusalem, who had retired to a nearby convent. The interior has three naves with elegantly capitalled columns on top of which are vaulted arches. In the crypt opening below, a Baroque altar commemorates the birth of Mary.

THE VIA DOLOROSA

Legend has it that almost immediately after the crucifixion of Jesus, his followers began to retrace his steps to Calvary. The term «Via Dolorosa» («The Way of Sorrows») was popularized in the 16th century and its fourteen stations were standardized by the Franciscans during the 19th century. This route, followed by the world's orthodox Christians, led from the Antonia Fortress, where Jesus appeared before Pilate and was condemned, out to Calvary (called Golgotha in Greek), which was outside the city walls at that time. (Alternate site: The Garden Tomb. See below).

First Station - The Chapel of the Flagellation where tradition holds that Jesus was interrogated by Pilate. The Franciscans begin their weekly procession through the Stations of the Cross here, on Friday afternoons. This modest chapel was built on the site of a Crusader oratory. Inside are glass panels representing the scourging of Jesus (center), Pilate cleansing his hands of the «blood of the innocent» (left), and the liberation of Barabas (right). On the dome above the altar is a large crown of golden thorns perforated by stars.

Ecce Homo Arch - This is the second station along the Via Dolorosa. In the 16th century, pilgrims began to refer to the arch as the Ecce Homo Arch, referring to Pilate's

declaration as he presented Jesus to the crowd of spectators, «Behold the man!». In reality it is part of a triumphal arch built by Hadrian in 135 A.D. to commemorate his conquest of Jerusalem. The original arch had three parts: the largest, central arch which spans the Via Dolorosa, the left arch which is no longer in existence, and the right arch that can still be seen today inside the Church of the Sisters of Zion.

The Struthion Pools - One of the Struthion Pools, originally built during the reign of the Hasmonean king Hyrcanus I (2nd century BC), it was partially destroyed by Herod when he built a moat around his Antonia Fortress and was later given a vaulted ceiling by Hadrian (135 A.D.).

Church of the Sisters of Zion - Here in this church are the remains of an ancient Roman pavement, the «Lithostratos». Drawings for dice games can still be seen etched in some of the slabs. Christian tradition has it that Roman soldiers played dice for Jesus' garments, and dice similar to those depicted in the drawings have actually been found.

Third Station - A small chapel built by Polish Catholic cavalrymen marks the spot where Jesus fell for the first time. The chapel belongs to the Armenian Catholic Patriarchate.

Fourth Station - A bas-relief sculpture by Zieliensky indicates the place where Jesus met his mother.

Fifth Station - As the inscription above the door of this Franciscan chapel says, here Simon of Cyrene took the cross from Jesus and carried it on to Golgotha. This is mentioned in three Gospels, but not in that of John.

Sixth Station - The Armenian Orthodox church here recalls Veronica who wiped the brow of Jesus with her veil. The impression of His face remained on the veil which has been kept in St. Peter's since 707. Inside the church is the tomb of St. Veronica.

Seventh Station - Here the Via Dolorosa intersects the noisy bazaar, and a column marked with the Roman numerals VII indicates where Jesus fell for the second time.

Eighth Station - A small plaque with a cross on the wall marks the place where Jesus met the pious women of Jerusalem and told them, «Don't weep for me, daughters of Jerusalem, but for yourselves and your children.»

Ninth Station - A column near the Ethiopian monastery shows the place where Jesus fell for the third time. The last five stations of the Via Dolorosa are inside the Holy Sepulchre.

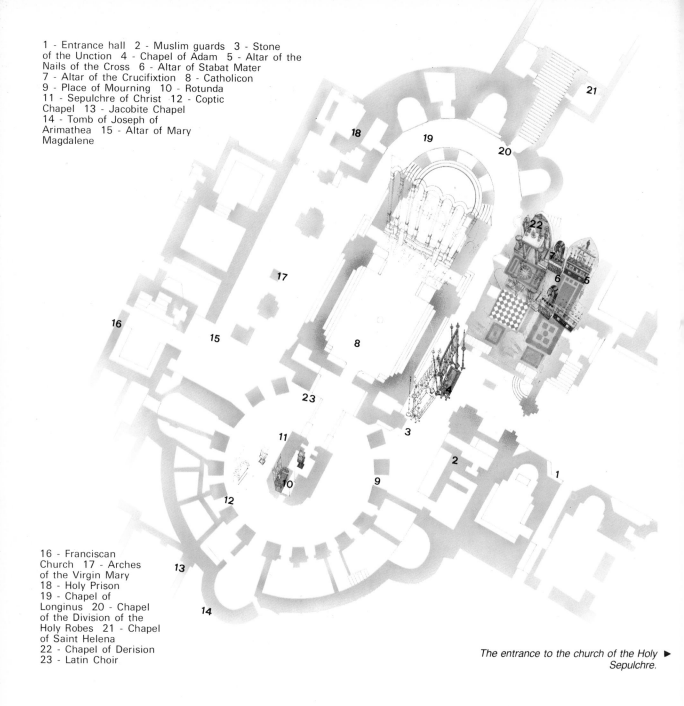

1 - Entrance hall 2 - Muslim guards 3 - Stone of the Unction 4 - Chapel of Adam 5 - Altar of the Nails of the Cross 6 - Altar of Stabat Mater 7 - Altar of the Crucifixtion 8 - Catholicon 9 - Place of Mourning 10 - Rotunda 11 - Sepulchre of Christ 12 - Coptic Chapel 13 - Jacobite Chapel 14 - Tomb of Joseph of Arimathea 15 - Altar of Mary Magdalene

16 - Franciscan Church 17 - Arches of the Virgin Mary 18 - Holy Prison 19 - Chapel of Longinus 20 - Chapel of the Division of the Holy Robes 21 - Chapel of Saint Helena 22 - Chapel of Derision 23 - Latin Choir

The entrance to the church of the Holy ▶ Sepulchre.

THE HOLY SEPULCHRE

The Church of the Holy Sepulchre is the most sacred site to Orthodox Christianity in Jerusalem. The quarry here was once an execution grounds outside the city's gates, with a hill plainly visible to everyone travelling to or from the city. It was called Golgotha, from the Hebrew word «golgolet», or «skull», which is what the hill resembled. In addition, there is a legend that Adam was buried here. Near Golgotha were many stone tombs which had been hewn into the surrounding bedrock. The area was incorporated by the Emperor Hadrian into his new city, Aelia Capitolina, as a Forum and Temple area, dedicated to Jupiter, Juno and Venus. Hadrian built this new pagan city over the ruins of Jerusalem, which he had completely destroyed in retaliation for a major Jewish revolt. (It was also at this time that he changed the name of the country from Israel/Judea to Palestine.)

Fortunately, Hadrian didn't level the rocks into which the tombs were dug for the construction of his Capitoline Temple. Instead, he limited himself to filling those spaces and leveling them off by placing large quantities of earth

The altar of the Nails of the Cross, on Golgotha.

*To the right, the small altar called Stabat ▶
Mater, and next to it, that of the
Crucifixtion, with the life size icons of
Christ, the Virgin and John.*

around' them. By doing so, he created a base for the temple, an enormous terrace that preserved the tombs from destruction.

In 331 A. D., the mother of Constantine the Great, Helena, and Bishop Macarius, travelled to the Holy Land to find Jesus' birthplace, tomb and other places important to Christianity. The excavations that the empress carried out here revealed the tomb of Jesus, His cross and those of the two thieves. Constantine had all the rocks and earth removed to expose Golgotha, where he placed a cross covered by a tabernacle, and the tomb, which he enclosed in a hugh rotunda called the «Anastasis», meaning Resurrection. The work was completed in 335 A. D. The basilica which stood east of the rotunda was destroyed by the Persians in 614. Reconstruction began 15 years later under the abbot Modestus and the church remained intact until the caliph El-Hakim had it totally razed in 1009.

When the Crusaders entered the city on July 15, 1099, they found the church as it had been reconstructed by the Emperor Constantine Monomachus. As it did not seem suitable to them, they took on the task of rebuilding the church almost entirely. The new edifice was completed in 1149. A ferocious fire devastated much of the church in 1808, but the western world, preoccupied with Napoleon in Europe, virtually ignored pleas for assistance in reconstructing it. The Greek Orthodox assumed control of the church and its repair, hence its present, predominantly eastern character.

Today, the inside of the Holy Sepulchre is divided among five communities: Roman Catholic, Greek Orthodox and Armenian (who together control most of the church), Copts and Syrian Orthodox. The Ethiopian monks have their cells and chapel on the roof of the church.

30

Golgotha - The Golgotha of today, accessible by steep steps, has two chapels side by side, one Roman Catholic and the other Greek Orthodox. On the Roman side are two Stations: where Jesus was stripped of his garments and where he was nailed to the cross. On the Greek side, the 12th Station: where Jesus died on the cross. Under the altar can be seen the top of the rocky outcrop with a silver marker where it is believed the cross stood. In between the two is the Stabat Mater, («Sorrowful Mother») in remembrance of Mary's agony at her son's death.

The Annointing Stone - Here tradition has it that Jesus was laid when he was taken down from the cross. His body was sprinkled with a mixture of myrrh and aloe and he was mourned by his mother before being laid in the tomb. This is the 13th Station of the Cross.

The Tomb - The edicule, the artificial structure that stands in the center of the anastasis, simulates the original two-roomed tomb of hewn stone. One enters the first room, the *Chapel of the Angel*, where a richly ornamented cube of marble is encased. It is believed to have been part of the tomb cover on which the angel was seated when the women came to annoint Jesus' body on Sunday morning and found the tomb empty. The second room is the mortuary chamber and the last station of the Via Dolorosa. A white marble slab about two yards long covers the bathtub type tomb which had been donated by Joseph of Arimathea. Above the tomb are 43 hanging lamps: four belonging to the Copts and the others equally divided among the Latins, Greeks and Armenians. An icon of the Virgin conceals part of the primitive rock tomb.

General view of the entrance to the Holy Sepulchre, with the Stone of the Unction in the foreground.

General view of the tomb of Christ.

The small space preserving the ▶ tombstone of the tomb of Christ.

Katholikon - This is the main body of the basilica, containing the inconostasis, the heavily decorated partition which separates the altar from the rest of the congregation. The large omphalos dome rises above the transept; it marks what many Christians consider to be «the center of the world».

Holy Prison - This narrow space, known also as the Prison of Christ, is really an ancient jail annexed to the Aelia Capitolina. Tradition identifies it as the jail in which Jesus spent the night after his arrest in Gethsemane.

Chapel of Saint Helena - This lower level chapel is dedicated to the mother of Constantine. It was built by the Crusaders and still rests on four 11th century columns. The chapel belongs to the Armenians.

Tomb of Joseph of Arimathea - This is the only part of the Holy Sepulchre belonging to the Ethiopian community. It is a small, rock-hewn tomb in the wall of the rotunda. Joseph of Arimathea, a wealthy member of the Sanhedrin, owned the tomb into which Jesus was laid, and was called «a good and just man who was waiting for the reign of God».

The iconostasis in the Katholikon and the dome over the crossing seen from below.

The interior of Christ's prison.

The rock excavated form the Tomb of
Joseph of Arimathea.

The beautiful crypt of St. Helena.

Church of Saint Mark - A 7th century chapel already existed on this spot, which was then restored by the Crusaders. The actual 19th century church of Syrian-Orthodox denomination is part of the Jacobite convent.

Church of Saint James - This is an Armenian-Orthodox church of which the actual state is due to the renovation of an 11th century construction. It was built in memory of the martyrdom of James the Great, brother of the evangelist John: James was beheaded here in 44 A.D. under orders of Herod the Great and ruler of Palestine from 41 to 44. His persecution of the Christians was dictated by the fact that he wanted to earn the position of priest. The richly ornamented interior conserves stones from sacred locations in the history of Israel: the Sinai, the Tabor, and the Jordan.

Church of Saint John the Baptist - The domes and bell towers of Jerusalem soar up against the blue skies and over the rooftops of Jerusalem. The one dedicated to John the Baptist, of Greek-Orthodox denomination, was built in the 11th century above a crypt.

Church of St. Mary Magdalene - Easily identifiable by its brilliant, onion-shaped gold domes, this White Russian Orthodox church was built between 1885 and 1888 by the Czar Alexander III in memory of his mother, Mary Alexandrova. Inside are many beautiful icons and the tomb of the Grand Duchess Elizabeth Feodorovna, who was assassinated in 1918.

Exterior and interior of the Church of St. Mark.

Exterior of the Church of St. James. ▶

The domes of the Russian Church of St. Mary ▶
Magdalene.

The bell-tower of the Church of St. John ▶
the Baptist amidst the roofs of Jerusalem.

Market - The streets of Jerusalem are full of twists and turns. Here one can buy anything because the market sells everything: colorful Arab clothing and headdresses, olive wood carvings, pieces of antique amber, perfumed spices and religious articles.

City of David - Just outside the Dung Gate of the Old City is the village of Silwan (Siloam). It covers the hillside (called in the Bible «Ophel») down to the Kidron Valley. This is where Jerusalem originated five thousand years ago. The well-marked excavations of Area G show the visitor many levels of the ancient city, from the Canaanite, through the Israelite up to the Hasmonean period. One follows the path down to the Warren's Shaft, where one actually enters the three-thousand year old Jebusite tunnel leading to a vertical shaft through which the ancient dwellers drew their water in times of siege. At the bottom of the hill, in the Kidron Valley itself, is the famous **Gihon Spring** where Solomon was crowned king. Here is the entrance to **Hezekiah's Tunnel**, an incredible feat of engineering which channeled the waters of the Gihon through the rock under the City of David into the Pool of Siloam where they were accessible to the city's inhabitants. The Tunnel was built by King Hezekiah in 701 B.C. An ancient Hebrew inscription found here (and removed to Istambul by the Turks) described the momentous project of digging the tunnel.

Two typical streets of Jerusalem's market, in the old city.

The Valley of the Kidron.
On the left is the pillar of Absalom,
the tomb of James and the tomb of Zacharias.
The so-called Pillar of Absalom (Right).

Kidron Valley - Just one look at the Valley of Kidron from the top of the Mount of Olives is sufficient to understand why this place has impressed the population of Jerusalem since ancient times. The harshness of the landscape, the scarce vegetation, the graves dug into the bedrock or isolated among the olive trees give this place an air of timelessness. Popular belief says that here, the Final Resurrection and Final Judgement will take place. One version says that a fine wire will be strung from the Old City wall across the valley to the Mount of Olives, and everyone must walk across. The good will make it to the end and the sinners will fall off into the valley.

Three monumental tombs on the valley floor catch the eye. One is the **Pillar of Absalom**, the rebellious son of David who, «had this monument built while he was still alive, saying: 'Not having sons, this will be the record of my name' and he named it after himself, and today it is still called the Hand of Absalom» (Kings II, 18:18). This monument has a Greek-style conical top which is called a «ptolos». Near it is the tomb of Zacharia (or St. James) with a pyramidal top, and in between is the catacomb tomb of the Ben Hasir family. All three date back to the Hellenistic period.

The hill dotted with olive trees that descend below the site of the Temple.

Exterior of the Church of the Tomb of Mary.

Church of the Tomb of Mary - The church's spare lines go back to the age of the Crusaders (11th century) and is of Greek-Orthodox denomination. Its interior houses the tombs of Anna and Joachim, parents of Mary and that of her husband Joseph as well. The rock-tomb of the Virgin is found in a crypt, enriched with icons, precious lamps and paintings.

The tombstone has three large holes in it permitting worshippers to touch the inside of Mary's tomb. It should not be forgotten however, that another tomb of the Virgin exists at Ephesus in Turkey: in fact, according to another version of the story, the apostle John took the mother of Jesus with him to Ephesus, where she remained until her death.

Gethsemane: the Church of all Nations and above, the Church of St. Mary Magdalene.

In the garden near the Church of all Nations are olive trees so old and contorted that they are considered to be direct descendants (if not the actual trees) of those that grew here in Jesus' time.

Views of the facade;
the mosaic on the main
altar with the rock, and
a detail of the crown of thorns.

The tunnel of the Pool of Siloah.

A detail of Gihon Spring.

Gethsemane - Church of All Nations - The name is derived from the Hebrew term for olive press, «gat shemen». Jesus endured his agony in the garden here before he was arrested. A sanctuary was built on the spot in the 4th century and later enlarged by the Crusaders. The present church, with its large, luminous mosaic in the tympanum, was built by the Italian Antonio Barluzzi between 1919 and 1924 on the remains of the previous structures. Inside, on the ceiling are the crests of nations who contributed to the church's construction. On the floor in front of the chalice-shaped altar is a crown of hammered steel thorns encircling a piece of rock where Jesus is believed to have knelt in prayer. The mosaic over the altar represents «*Christ in Agony*», those in the lateral apses are titled «*The Kiss of Judas*» and «*Christ's Arrest*».

Pool of Siloah - The pool of Siloah or Siloam, nestled at the lower end of the Tyropean Valley at the end of Hezekiah's Tunnel, holds the memory of Jesus' healing of the blind man, «Go bathe in the pool of Siloah» (John 9:7).

The Gihon Spring - Approach to the Gihon Spring. This was Jerusalem's primary water source in ancient times. When the Assyrians threatened the city, Judean king Hezekiah built his famous tunnel (701 B. C.) to convey water from the spring to the Siloam Pool, safe within the city walls.

◄ *The splendid panorama of Jerusalem as enjoyed from the window of the Dominus Flevit.*

The rock-hewn tomb.

◄ *Gardens and walls at the Garden Tomb.*

Church of Dominus Flevit - Here Jesus, nearing Jerusalem, stopped and wept over the destiny that awaited the city: «...and they won't leave you a stone standing because you haven't acknowledged the moment in which you have been visited».

The present church belongs to the Franciscans and was built by Barluzzi in the late 1930's over the ruins of a 5th century church. Remains of an ancient necropolis were discovered in the area, revealing numerous Hebrew, Aramic and Greek epitaphs. Absolutely unforgettable is the view of Jerusalem from the window over the altar.

Garden Tomb - Often called «Gordon's Calvary» after the British officer who first saw the site from the top of Damascus Gate, this rocky outcrop and garden around it contain an ancient tomb which many Christians believe to have been the sepulchre of Jesus. From many angles, the hill resembles a skull, and there are various other features about the garden (e.g., large cistern, wine press, location near city gate) which make it a plausible alternate site to the Holy Sepulchre. Its serene atmosphere and lovely gardens are, for many, much more conducive to prayer and contemplation. Free guided tours are conducted on request. The Garden Tomb is administered by the Garden Tomb Association founded and based in England.

45

Exterior and interior of the tomb of Lazarus.

*On the next page, the chapel of the ►
Ascension and the Church of St. Peter in Gallicantu.*

Tomb of Lazarus - It is written in the Gospel of St. John:
« There was an ill man, a certain Lazarus of Bethany, the
village of Mary and Martha, his sister... Bethany was
about fifteen furlongs from Jerusalem ».

Today the village of Bethany is called Azariyeh in
Arabic, after the ancient Lazarion of Byzantine times.
Lazarus' tomb, today property of the Moslems, is reached
by descending 24 steep steps put there in the 17th century. Here, the body of Lazarus was resuscitated by the
words of Jesus.

Church of the Ascension - According to the Gospels, Jesus reappeared to the apostles forty days after the Resurrection and took them to the top of the Mount of Olives and «...while he blessed them, he separated himself from them and ascended up into Heaven». Here then, the earthly life of Christ was concluded. The supernatural event is remembered here by a 13th century chapel belonging to the Moslems for whom, it must be remembered, Jesus was one of the great prophets.

This chapel originally had a double, circular portico and open arcades. Now the small round building houses the rock with a footprint said to be that of Jesus from the moment of his ascension.

Church of Saint Peter in Gallicantu - The name given to this church records the episode in which Peter denied the Master three times after the crow of the rooster. The actual church, consecrated in 1931 and belonging to the Assumptionists of Catholic denomination, rises over the ruins of a pre-existent Byzantine basilica. Someone has hypothesised that this was the site of the house of the High Priest Caiaphas, but it has not as of yet been confirmed. What has been brought to light meanwhile, is a beautiful street of steps called the maccabean stairs, which in the first century A. D. must have joined Mount Zion to the valley of the Kidron.

The slender, pointed arches of the Coenaculum.

The exterior of the Church of the ▶
Dormition at sunset and the crypt with the
statue of Mary sleeping.

Coenaculum - On top of Mount Zion is the Coenaculum, or Room of the Last Supper, where one of the most momentous events in the Christian faith occurred: the institution of the Eucharist. Also, seven weeks later, the Holy Spirit appeared here to Mary and the apostles during the Pentecost. The Crusaders built the present room with its beautiful pointed arches, but in the 15th century, the Moslems took possession of Mount Zion, transforming the church into a mosque and prohibiting both Christians and Jews from entering for nearly five centuries.

Church of the Dormition - This is a Benedictine church designed by Heinrich Renard and built at the turn of the century in Romanesque style with a domed bell tower. Here, Mary fell into an «eternal sleep». The church crypt, in fact, contains a statue of Mary, reclining, caught in her final slumber.

The grand sarcophagus of the tomb of David.

*General view of the Israel Museum and ▶
the outside of the Shrine of the Book.*

Tomb of David - Since the 10th century it has been thought that King David, after his 40-year reign over Israel, was probably buried here, although it is more likely that he was buried on the Ophel with other Israelite kings. A church was built here in the 4th century and was later restored by the Crusaders. In 1524, the Moslems, who venerate El Nabi Daoud as a great prophet, turned this site into a mosque and prohibited Jews and Christians from entering until 1948.

The large stone cenotaph, covered by an ornate cloth featuring the Star of David, has several silver crowns, decorations for the Torah scrolls, symbolizing the kings of Judah who succeeded David.

Israel Museum - Inaugurated in 1965, it was designed by two Israeli architects, Alfred Mansfeld and Dora Gad. It consists of several components whose modern lines fit in perfectly with the surrounding hills, dotted with olive and cypress trees. Its five pavillions are: the Bronfman Biblical and Archaeological Museum, the Bezabel Folk Art exhibit, the Billy Rose Sculpture Gardens, the Ruth Children's Museum and, most important, the *Shrine of the Book* wherein are the Dead Sea Scrolls, the two-thousand year-old biblical manuscripts found in caves at Qumran. The Shrine was designed by the Americans Frederik Kiesler and Armand Bartos. The white dome contrasts with the black basalt wall, symbolizing the envisioned battle between the Sons of Light (the Essenes) and the Sons of Darkness.

◀ *The exterior of the Russian church.*

◀ *A suggestive framing of the tomb of Sanhedrin.*

The interior of the Great Synagogue.

Russian Church - Beautiful green domes topped by golden crosses characterize Jerusalem's Russian-Orthodox church. An enormous stone column 12 yards long lays on the ground in front of it: probably broken off during construction work on the Temple of Herod. During the British mandate of Israel, English authorities occupied part of the convent's apartments transforming them into offices.

Tombs of the Sanhedrin - Also known as the Tombs of the Judges, they are a series of rock catacombs hewn into three separate levels. For the most part, they go back to the 6th century A. D. but some are also from the Maccabean period. Tradition says that members of the Sanhedrin, the Supreme Court and highest religious authority of Temple times, are buried here. The head of the Sanhedrin was the Nasi, or prince, whose position was usually inherited.

Great Synagogue - This is the biggest and most modern synagogue in Israel. Next to it is the synagogue of the Chief Rabbinate of Israel, or Heikhal Shlomo, where Jewish prayer services are held both in the Ashkenazi (European) style and in the Sephardi (North African) style. Inside the synagogue is a beautiful 17th century Ark from Padua, Italy. There is a museum, called Dor va Dor (Generation to Generation), which includes the reconstruction of an old Italian synagogue.

The famous stained-glass windows by Marc Chagall in the Synagogue of the Hadassah Hospital.

Knesset - The Israeli National Assembly has its headquarters in this building which was inaugurated in 1966. Its construction was financed by James Rothchild and the artists Marc Chagall, Dani Karavan and David Palumbo contributed their works. The Knesset is composed of 120 members who are elected every four years. Facing the main entrance of the building is the large bronze menorah (seven-branched candelabrum), decorated with 29 scenes from the history of Israel. It is the work of the English sculptor Benno Elkian and was a gift of the British Parliament.

Convent of the Cross - Surrounded by a very high wall, the Convent of the Cross rose over a primitive 6th century construction, fortified in its day, — the 11th century, — by Georgians from Caucasus. The tradition says that Lot, escaping the destruction of Sodom, settled here and planted a tree from which the wood was made for the cross of Jesus. Even today, behind the main altar, there is a ring of silver marking the spot where legend says the tree grew.

Hadassah Hospital - Here in Ein Kerem is one of the most beautiful works of art of our day: the stained glass windows by Marc Chagall which were installed and dedicated in the hospital in 1961. The twelve panels, whose colors match those of the breastplate of the High Priest described in the Book of Exodus, represent Jacob's parting words to his twelve sons. These twelve sons were to become most of the twelve tribes of Israel (Joseph was not a tribe, but his two sons, Ephraim and Menashe, were to become half-tribes). With his assistant, Charles Marc, Chagall developed a special technique of using up to three colors in each panel, whereas before, each bit of stained glass had to be isolated by borders of lead.

Yad Vashem - This is a place of commemoration and homage to the six million Jewish victims of the Nazi regime. There are many components of Yad Vashem, including a museum which documents the rise of Hitler's National Socialist Party, the deeds it perpetrated during World War II and the aftermath. Outside there is a towering column dedicated to the memory of all those who resisted Nazism, with the word «Zkor» at the top, Remember. In the Ohel Yizkor, a low building made of unhewn boulders, the visitor will find the names of the major death camps written on the floor. An eternal flame burns next to a vault containing the ashes of some of those who died in the Holocaust.

Rockefeller Museum - Built with funds donated by John D. Rockefeller and designed by English architect Austin Harrison, this museum houses some of the most important archaeological finds in the country. It is an elegant construction of pink and white limestone with an octagonal tower and a courtyard pool around which the exhibit rooms are located.

The sanctuary of Yad Vashem.

The exterior and a room of the ▶ Rockefeller Museum.

A bas-relief in the square of Yad Vashem.

THE GHETTO UPRISING - THE LAST MARCH

Rachel's Tomb - The only one of the biblical matriarchs and patriarchs not buried in Hebron's Machpela Cave, Rachel died in childbirth here on the Bethlehem-Efrat road (Genesis 35:19-20). Her husband, Jacob, placed a marker on the spot. Still today, Rachel's tomb is a favorite site for prayer among Jews, particularly among those who encounter difficulty in bearing children.

BETHLEHEM

A few miles south of Jerusalem along a charming, biblical road, is the hilltop town of Bethlehem. The name Bethlehem has two meanings: in Hebrew, the House of Bread, and in Arabic, the House of Meat.

On both sides of the road are vast, rocky pastures where shepherds tend their flocks of sheep and goats. One of these is aptly called the «Shepherds' Fields» because here the angels announced the birth of Jesus. It was also in these fields that the tender love story between Ruth and Boaz unfolded as narrated in the Book of Ruth. Their son, Obed, was to become the grandfather of King David, who was born in Bethlehem a thousand years before the birth of Jesus. For Christians, Bethlehem is a holy city because

Jesus was born there. «In those days, an edict of Augustus came out for the census of the entire empire.» One of the principal functions of the Roman administration was to impose taxes. Therefore, the census ordered by Augustus, and supervised by the local governor Publius Sulpicius Quirinus, was certain to provide ready monies to the authorities. Since law decreed that every landowner had to declare his property for purposes of taxation, Joseph had to leave Nazareth and return to Bethlehem «...together with his bride, Mary, who was with child. While they were in that place, the moment of birth arrived and there she brought forth her firstborn son, wrapped him in swaddling clothes and laid him in a

Panorama of Bethlehem.

The tiny entrance to the basilica, called the 'door of humility'.

manger because there was no room for them at the inn». This is how the Gospel of Luke describes the event destined to change the history of mankind. The actual birthdate of Jesus is disputed: for Roman Catholics it is December 24, for Greek Orthodox it is January 6 and for the Armenians, January 18. In contempt for the pilgrims who had venerated this place since the earliest times, Emperor Hadrian, in 135 A. D., consecrated the woods and caves here to Adonis and introduced his own pagan cult. In 332, Constantine the Great, after having the woods cut down, ordered the construction of a basilica on the spot. The present structure is a combination of Constantine's basilica (much of which was destroyed two

The interior of the Basilica of the Nativity.

A detail of the silver star that marks ▶
the birthplace of Jesus.

The grotto of the Nativity with the altar ▶
of the birth of Christ and that of the crib.

centuries after its construction), Justin's sixth century renovations and later Crusader repairs. The basilica was miraculously spared during the Persian invasion of 614, because the invaders found a painting of the three Magi, whom they took to be Persians, decorating the pediment.

In 1101, Baldwin I was crowned Crusader king there, and twenty years later, Baldwin II and his wife were, as well. Then came a long decline. In 1646, the Turks melted down the lead from its roof to make cannonballs. About the same time, the Christian community decided to block up the main entrance except for a very small opening, to prevent the locals from riding into the church on horseback. The door is only one and a half yards high, and is sometimes called the «gate of humility» since one has to stoop to enter.

Inside the basilica, red limestone columns with

Corinthian capitals line the double aisles on either side of the central nave. Above them, one sees the remnants of mosaics, done in 1169, which have a gold background and depict the ancestors of Jesus and the first seven ecumenical councils. Of these councils, only the first at Constantinopole has survived in its entirety, while fragments of the others, Nicaea, Ephesus and Chalcedon, can also be seen.

The Chapel of the Nativity - This is the small grotto located directly under the main altar of the church. In its small apse a silver star marks the place of Jesus' birth. Above the altar are fifteen lamps belonging to different Christian communities. In a sunken chapel off to the side of the grotto are two altars: the *altar of the crib* where the newborn infant was laid, and the *altar of the Magi*, the three kings who came to worship the newborn king.

The cloister of the Church of St.
Catherine, with the statue of St. Jerome.

The interior of the Church of St.
Catherine, where Christmas mass is
celebrated.

A corner of the cloister of the Church of St. Catherine.

St. Catherine's - Next door to the Church of the Nativity is the Roman Catholic church of St. Catherine. It was built by the Franciscans in 1881 over a cave where, tradition says, St. Jerome lived when he was translating the scriptures from the Greek Septuagint to the Latin Vulgate in the 4th century. A statue of him can be seen in the courtyard, once part of a Crusader cloistered convent, outside. St. Catherine's is where Christmas Midnight Mass is celebrated and relayed throughout the world via satellite.

Panorama of Ein Karem and the interior
of the grotto where John the Baptist
was born.

EIN KAREM

This small village, a western suburb of Jerusalem since 1961, is the biblical Beit Hakerem, «Fountain of the Vineyard». Inhabited by Arabs, it was abandoned in 1948 and resettled by Jewish immigrants in the 1950s. This was the scene of the Visitation, when Mary went to see her cousin Elizabeth, who greeted the future mother of Jesus with the words, «Blessed art thou among women». Mary responded with the «Magnificat», a song of praise to the Lord, inscribed in the Church of the Visitation, built in 1939 by Antonio Barluzzi.

Ein Karem is the birthplace of St. John the Baptist. A fifth-century Franciscan monastery dedicated to him was built on the traditional site of the home of his parents, Elizabeth and Zachary. It was used as a stable by the Arabs but later restored. In the crypt is the **Grotto of Benedictus**, the presumed birthplace of John the Baptist. A marble star in front of the altar recalls the event with these words: «Hic precursor Domini natus est».

HEBRON

Hebron, probably one of the oldest cities in the world, is situated in the Judean hills. Long famous for its fertility, this area inspired Moses' scouts to describe the Promised Land as «flowing with milk and honey». According to the Bible, Hebron was the home of a race of giants: «The land through which we have gone to search it, is a land that eateth up the inhabitants thereof; and all the people that we saw in it are men of great stature. And there we saw the giants, the sons of Anak, which come of the giants» (Numbers 13:32-33).

The ancient name of Hebron is Kiryat Arba, which means «City of the Four» (four neighboring confederated settlements). History has left a deep impression on Hebron, known as the home of Adam, the first territorial possession of the nomad Abraham, who is buried there with his wife and descendants, and also the capital of the kingdom of David for seven years.

The Tombs of the Patriarchs in Hebron: inside are the tombs of Abraham and his wife Sarah, Isaac and Rebecca, Jacob and Leah.

Hebron is holy to Moslems as well as Jews, since the former also consider themselves to be descendants of Abraham. In Arabic, Hebron is known as «El Khalil» («Friend (of God))», a name given to Abraham. Tension between the Moslem and Jewish communities resulted in bloody outbursts in which many Jews were massacred between 1929 and 1936. The British evacuated the Jews to Jerusalem, and the Jordanian administration subsequently prohibited them from returning to Hebron. After 1967, Jewish settlement was revived. At present, both Moslem and Jewish worshippers gather at the **Haram El-Khalil**, the Moslem shrine which contains the tombs of the patriarchs. But the tensions between the two peoples persist.

JERICHO

Ancient Jericho, which was first settled in the eighth millennium B.C., lies 250 meters below sea level and is situated at what is now known as Tel Al-Sultan. Remains of defensive city walls and an impressive stone tower from this period can still be seen. Jericho is best known from the biblical account of Joshua, who caused the walls to fall by blowing shofars (ram's horn trumpets). According to the Book of Kings, the Prophet Elijah cured the «bitter» waters of Ein Al-Sultan, the spring there, with salt (II Kings 2:21). Modern Jericho is located nearly two kilometers to the south, where the Byzantine town of Jericho once stood.

Objects in blown glass are one of the typical local craft products.

One of the most interesting evidences of the antiquity of Jericho: the nine-meter high rampart, the foundations of which date to 7000 B.C.

Two details of the sumputuous ▶ palace of Hisham, a few kilometers from Jericho.

QUMRAN

The remains of a monastic settlement inhabited by an ancient Hebrew sect, the Essenes, have come to light in an apocalyptically beautiful landscape on the northwest shore of the Dead Sea. The Essenes lived there in communal style between the second century B. C. and 68 A. D., the year in which Vespasian's Tenth Legion occupied the area and scattered the members of the sect. The Essene doctrines and rites were surprisingly similar to those of the early Christians. Of chief importance was to live a life of purity and asceticism far from the pomp and magnificence of Jerusalem. The followers of «The Teacher of Righteousness», as the founder of the sect was called, took refuge in the desert, where they lived in poverty and divided the fruits of their labors equally among themselves. They performed purifying rites such as baptism

and frequent ablutions and studied the Holy Scriptures as they awaited the imminent end of the world.

Meals, which were eaten communally, had a sacred character. The dining room was purified with water, quite extraordinary when the extreme aridity of the area is taken into consideration. But the ancient inhabitants of Qumran were well organized from this point of view. A clever network of channels and cisterns, fed by an aqueduct from the western hills, provided water to all parts of the settlement. Rooms used for various purposes have been identified: kitchens, storerooms, workshops, a refectory, and the scriptorium, in which the famous Dead Sea Scrolls were written. Some of the scrolls were found by chance in 1947 in a cave near the settlement ruins. They had been wrapped in linen and placed in carefully sealed

The ruins of the ancient settlement of Qumran are situated on a rocky spur that dominates the Dead Sea.

jars, an indication that whoever hid them did all in his power to preserve them. This first discovery led to further exploration of surrounding caves, which yielded hundreds of manuscripts. These, however, must have been more hastily hidden, because they were not as carefully protected, probably due to the sudden dispersion of the Essenes.

The manuscripts, most written in Hebrew and some in Aramaic, date back about a thousand years earlier than the oldest examples of the Hebrew Scriptures known up to 1947. They contain all of the Old Testament texts except Esther, and also include the Deuterocanons, the Apocrypha, and writings in which the rules and doctrines of the Qumran community are described.

The Dead Sea: saline formations, an example of how easy it is to float, and the famous mud baths, outstanding for health and beauty treatments.

The road signs indicate sea level. The Dead Sea itself is at the lowest point on the earth's surface, 398 meters below sea level.

DEAD SEA

Saline formations crop up from the water like ghostly coral, and the rocky landscape is scorched by an implacable sun in a motionless, blinding sky. Nature reveals all of its calcified wrinkles and seems to be eternally punished by the torrent of fire with which God damned it. There is no life to be found in the water, and all life on the land must adapt to this terrible blasting furnace of salt.

The Dead Sea, the biblical Salt Sea, lies at the bottom of the Great Syrian African Rift Valley, about 400 meters (1280 feet) below sea level. This remnant of the sea, which covered the area over two million years ago, is the lowest point on the face of the earth. Its depth ranges from 430 meters (1376 feet) in the north to 10 meters (32 feet) in the south. Its atmospheric pressure is higher than that of any

other site, and there is 15% more oxygen in the air there than over the Mediterranean. Due to a very high rate of evaporation, the water of this lake has a salt content of over 30%, nearly ten times the salinity of normal sea water. Consequently, the water is extremely dense, and swimmers find it very easy to float in the Dead Sea.

The water is laden with considerable quantities of other minerals that give it a bitter taste and oily consistency. When bathing in the Dead Sea, the swimmer should be careful to keep the water out of his eyes. The Dead Sea is famous for its therapeutic properties and is particularly effective in the treatment of skin disorders. The dry, oxygen-rich air is also valuable in the treatment of respiratory ailments.

MASADA

The mountain fortress of Masada looms over this magnificently desolate landscape on the edge of the Dead Sea. The name rings out as a warning and a promise in the phrase «Masada shall not fall again», recited by many Israeli fighting units when they take their oath of allegiance at the site. Following the destruction of the Temple in Jerusalem in 70 A. D., a remnant of Jewish rebels ascended the mountain, took over the Herodian fortress, and withstood a three-year Roman siege. The end came only when the Roman commander, Flavius Silva, had an enormous access ramp constructed on the west side of the mountain, enabling his army to reach the fortifications. On the eve of the final Roman attack, one of the most moving tragedies in the history of mankind took place within the walls. For fear of Roman retaliation and dreading above all the idea of slavery for the members of their families, the combatants of Masada chose suicide

The cableway which connects Masada to the plain; the evocative landscape of the Dead Sea seen from the ruins; a detail of the storerooms of the old citadel.

On this page: an arch, the tower which overlooks the storerooms, a corner of Herod's palace and the Baths.

over being taken alive by the enemy.

The contemporary historian, Josephus Flavius, describes their last moments:

«While they caressed and embraced their wives and held their children aloft in their arms weeping and kissing them for the last time, at the same time, as if it were someone else who was acting, they effected their plan, consoling themselves with the thought of the tortures they would have suffered had they fallen into the enemy hands. In the end there was not one who did not rise to the occasion and all killed their dear ones, one after the other... Then, unable to bear the anguish of what they had done and feeling they would offend the dead if they continued to live, they hastened to pile their belongings in a simple pile and set fire to it; then having chosen lots as to which of them would kill all the others, they lay down next to the bodies of their wives and children and embraced them as they bared their throats to those charged with killing them. After having killed all of them without wavering, the survivors once more drew lots and the one chosen by fate was to kill the other nine and finally himself... At the end the nine bared their throats to their companion who, when he was sole survivor, first looked around to see if in that slaughter there was anyone left who needed him; then when he was certain all were dead, he set fire to the palace, and gathering together whatever strength remained, plunged his sword into his body up to its hilt and fell down heavily next to his relatives» (Josephus Flavius, *History of the Jewish Wars*, VII, 8:6-8). Thus the last bulwark of the Jewish revolt fell. When the Romans managed to get through the smoking ruins they found nothing but 960 lifeless bodies awaiting them.

A large archaeological expedition, led by Professor Yigal Yadin, uncovered over 90% of the site between 1963 and 1965. Not only the ancient fortress, but also numerous buildings, palaces, storerooms and water facilities were excavated. Before the Jewish Revolt, Masada had been fortified by the Hasmoneans and subsequently converted into a luxurious stronghold by King Herod. It was meant to be a refuge for him in the event of a revolt or in case Cleopatra's expansionist policies succeeded. Today we can admire his magnificent palaces and the enormous cisterns he excavated in the rock to ensure an ample water supply.

The lower terrace of Herod's palace and the ruins which dominate the Dead Sea.

Traces of the encampment set up by the Roman legion when they laid siege to the fortress are clearly visible in the superb landscape which surrounds Masada.

The imposing access ramp built by the ▶ Romans seen from the side and from above: this was the only way to overcome the resistence of Masada.

◄ *The large petrified pilaster of salt, known as «Lot's wife», near Sodom.*

Panorama of Tel Aviv, the «Hill of Spring».»

◄ *Two contrasting aspects of the landscape near Sodom: a wild goat among the rocks and a luxuriant oasis appearing in the midst of the desert.*

SODOM

Nothing remains of ancient Sodom. The only reminder of the biblical story of Sodom and Gomorrah is a rock that looks vaguely human: according to popular fantasy, this is Lot's unfortunate wife, transformed into a pillar of salt as she was fleeing with her husband and daughters from the rain of fire that God had sent down on Sodom (Gen. 19:26).

Today it is the site of the Dead Sea Works, which mine the area's deposits of potassium, magnesium, bromide and other minerals.

TEL AVIV

Tel Aviv was born at the beginning of the twentieth century as a modest urban settlement on the dunes to the north of Jaffa. It grew so fast that it swallowed up the neighboring city and together they now comprise a single great metropolis: Tel Aviv-Jaffa. In 1909, a group of Jewish immigrants in Jaffa acquired a stretch of barren land and began to build there, probably intending to create an urban complex more fitting to their needs. Their lifestyle was western and it was therefore difficult for them to adapt to the Arab character of Jaffa. The new settlement was first called «Ahuzat Beit» but later became known as Tel Aviv («Hill of Spring»). The name actually came from the Babylonian town were the prophet Ezekiel had his «vision of dry bones», wherein God breathed life into skeletons scattered on the ground. They stood up and returned to Zion. It was considered a fitting name for the first all Hebrew-speaking city in modern Israel. During the first half of the twentieth century, Tel Aviv's population swelled so rapidly that it became Israel's economic and cultural center. It was here that Israel's independence was proclaimed on May 14, 1948, in Mayor Meir Dizengoff's house, which had been a museum since 1930. Today, Tel Aviv is Israel's largest city. It was not developed according to any particular urban plan, and so its buildings display many different architectural styles. Functional architectural style, such as the Bauhaus, popularized during the thirties, is in evidence everywhere.

Dominating the city is the **Shalom Tower**, from the top of which one can admire Tel Aviv and all its suburbs.

Particularly of note are Bat Yam and Ramat Gan where sport facilities host Jewish athletes from all over the world every four years in the Maccabean Games. The cosmopolitan and cultural aspects of the Israeli metropolis come to life particularly at night, when people crowd into the nightclubs and cafes, theaters and concert halls. The famous Dizengoff Street and its Dizengoff Center are the meeting places for all Tel Avivians after sunset. Tel Aviv is the home of one of the world's greatest symphony orchestras, the Israel Philharmonic, as well as the famous Habimah Theater company. There are numerous cinemas, art galleries, repertory theaters, historical buildings and places of interest to visit, including the Great Synagogue, the Carmel Market, the **Shalom Tower**, the **Diaspora Museum** and Beit Hahaganah.

Shalom Tower, one of the modern buildings in the center of Tel Aviv.

The exterior and two rooms in the Diaspora Museum. In the foreground is a model of the Synagogue in Florence.

A detail of the excavations of Tel Qasila, where the remains of twelve cities built one on top of the other have come to light.

The exterior of the church of St. Peter, the artists' quarter by night and the Clock Tower.

TEL QASILA

The **Museum of Eretz Israel**, beyond the Yarkon River in northern Tel Aviv, is also of great interest. There are eleven pavilions in the complex, one of which houses the Ethnographic Museum with finds from nearby Tel Qasila. There, Prof. Meisler undertook important archaeological excavations in 1948 which were interrupted in 1959 and renewed in 1971. The twelve layers of civilization exposed at Tel Qasila showed that the site had been continuously inhabited from the Neolithic to the Early Arab period. These mute witnesses of vanished civilizations include the remains of three temples and an inscription dating to 400 A. D. The extraordinary vitality of this settlement, destroyed and repeatedly rebuilt, confirms the hypothesis that it was a trade center, situated along the Phoenician caravan trade route. The cedars of Lebanon may have reached Jerusalem via Tel Qasila, which was the thriving port city of Jaffa during the time of King Solomon. The Egyptians razed it to the ground and the kings of Israel rebuilt it in the ninth century B.C. The center was once more destroyed in 732 B.C. by an Assyrian king, but it rose again from its ashes to become, in turn, a center for the Hellenes, Romans, Byzantines, Moslems and Mamelukes. The artifacts found here show that the site's ancient inhabitants worked in agriculture, weaving, leather and pottery. Various kinds of terra-cotta pots have been unearthed as well as weapons, writing objects and a statuette of the goddess Astarte. Oddly, no written documents were found.

JAFFA (YAFO)

Today, an integral part of Tel Aviv, Jaffa is situated in the region Joshua gave to the tribe of Dan and it is one of the oldest cities in the world. The name recalls the Hebrew word for «beautiful» and according to tradition, it was named for Japhet, one of Noah's three sons. It served as a port for Jerusalem and it was from there that the prophet Jonah embarked for Tarshish. The ships laden with the famous cedars of Lebanon used by King Solomon to build his temple landed there. It was at Jaffa that the apostle Peter, guest of Simon the Tanner, resuscitated Tabitha. A Greek legend recounts that this is also the site of the rock to which the beautiful Andromeda was bound as a sacrifice to the sea monster but who was then saved from her terrible fate by Perseus.

History passed through Jaffa often, sometimes leaving death and destruction in its wake. Occupied by the Egyptians circa 3400 years ago, the port later was a coveted objective for all the armies that passed through Israel.

Destroyed by Napoleon in 1799, the town was rebuilt at the beginning of the 19th century. It was governed by the Ottomans until the British Mandate and not until 1948 did it return once more to Israel. A favorite with young Israeli artists, modern Jaffa has a wealth of stores, bars and restaurants, exhibitions and places to see, including the Great Mosque, the **Clock Tower**, the archaeological museum, the flea market, the **artists' quarter** and the fishing port.

ASHKELON

ASHKELON WAS ONE OF THE MOST ANCIENT TOWNS IN THE
LAND, FOUNDED PROBABLY IN THE THIRD MILLENNIUM B.C.E.
IT WAS THE CITY OF ONE OF THE FIVE PHILISTINE PRINCES.
"TELL IT NOT IN GATH, PUBLISH IT NOT IN THE STREETS OF
ASHKELON; LEST THE DAUGHTERS OF THE PHILISTINES
REJOICE, LEST THE DAUGHTERS OF THE UNCIRCUMCIZED
TRIUMPH." (DAVID'S LAMENT OVER SAUL AND JONATHAN — II
SAMUEL, I, 20).
THE CITY FLOURISHED DURING THE HELLENISTIC AND ROMAN
PERIODS, WHEN MANY BEAUTIFUL PUBLIC BUILDINGS WERE
CONSTRUCTED. SOME HAVE BEEN EXCAVATED. THE CITY
PLAYED AN IMPORTANT PART IN THE WAR BETWEEN THE
CRUSADERS AND THE MOSLEMS UNTIL ITS DESTRUCTION IN
1270 BY THE MAMELUKE SULTAN, BAYBARS.
THE PROPHET ZEPHANIAH FORETOLD THE RESTORATION OF
ASHKELON AS AN ISRAELITE CITY.
"AND THE COAST SHALL BE FOR THE REMNANT OF THE HOUSE
OF JUDAH; THEY SHALL FEED THEREUPON; IN THE HOUSES OF
ASHKELON SHALL THEY LIE DOWN IN THE EVENING; FOR THE
LORD THEIR GOD SHALL VISIT THEM, AND TURN AWAY THEIR
CAPTIVITY." (ZEPHANIAH II, 7)

On these pages, the excavations of Ashkelon, one of the most beautiful seaside resorts in Israel.

ASHKELON

A green oasis with splendid gardens and equipped with the most up-to-date tourist facilities, modern Ashkelon is now a pleasant town overlooking the Mediterranean, a favorite for lovers of seaside resorts. Once upon a time, however, it was a port on the Philistine coast and scene of interminable battles between the Philistines and Israelites. It was at Ashkelon that Samson lost his legendary strength when Delilah cut his hair. This may also have been the birthplace of King Herod the Great, who adorned the city with magnificent colonnades. Vestiges of these and other archaeological finds are preserved in the **Ashkelon National Park**. In the past, Ashkelon's strategic importance was such that rival armies repeatedly invaded it, clashed over it, destroyed and rebuilt it. The Mamelukes destroyed the port for the last and final time in 1279, and it disappeared, swallowed up by luxurious forest. The first archaeological excavations were begun in 1920. Today, Ashkelon has two distinct residential areas: the old city to the east known as Migdal, already inhabited by Arabs in the 19th century, and Afridar, a growing Israeli suburb along the coast.

CAESAREA

The name itself evokes visions of the ancient city at the dawn of the Christian era when Herod the Great dedicated it to Caesar. He adorned the city with fine marble and splendid monuments, the remains of which can still be seen. Many peoples and creeds were to govern the city throughout its history as an important coastal station. The Phoenicians founded a base there in the 4th century B. C. Long after the fall of Herod's city, it was fortified as a stronghold by the Crusaders who landed there in 1101. The remains of the walls and citadel built by Louis IX of France testify to the passage of the Christian warriors who restored the Holy Grail, the precious chalice with which, according to tradition, Christ instituted the sacrament of the Eucharist to Christianity during the Last Supper.

But the city's past is as full of tears and horror as it is rich in glory and memories. History was transmuted into tragedy in the magnificent arena of Caesarea when thousands of Hebrews were thrown to famished wild beasts as punishment for revolting against the Romans in 66 A. D. and again, with Bar Kochba, in 132 A. D.

Two views of the archaeological zone of Caesarea.

MEGIDDO

The tel of ancient Megiddo dominates one of the most important commercial and military crossroads of antiquity, the Derech Hayam of the Hebrew Scriptures which the Romans called the Via Maris. This was the route used by traders to connect the country's interior to the sea and was thus strategically important. All of the peoples in the area have fought to control it. Egyptians, Babylonians, Assyrians, Hittites, Canaanites, Hebrews, Persians, Greeks, Parthians, Romans, Byzantines, Arabs, Crusaders, Turks – all of them clashed in the Plain of Jezreel. Its fame as a place of battle echoes in the inspired pages of the Apocalypse of St. John where it is called Armageddon, site of the ultimate clash between the forces of Good and Evil: «And he gathered them together into a place called in the Hebrew tongue Armageddon.» (Rev. 16:16). Clear evidence of Megiddo's warlike past lies in its twenty strata of ruins, many of which were once military structures, all heaped one on top of the other.

The excavations at Megiddo and a detail of the tunnel dug to bring drinking water into the fortress.

Views of the Bahai Shrine. Baha'uk'llah, the founder of
this religion, is buried here.

The exterior of the Stella Maris monastery.

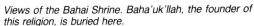 A panorama of the city and the Cave of the Elijah.

HAIFA

Haifa is located on the slopes of Mount Carmel overlooking the Mediterranean Sea. The city consists of three
levels: the highly industrialized shoreline, the middle
«Hadar» area half-way up the mountain, and the lovely
residential area on top called «Carmel». From here,
the eye sweeps over the splendid panorama of the entire
bay as far as Akko and, on clear days, up to the hills of the
Lebanese frontier. Painful memories are bound to the bay
of Haifa. During the British Mandate (1917-1948), the
publication of the 1939 White Paper severely limited
Jewish immigration into the country. Thousands of Jews
who were fleeing the Nazis were turned back from the
port of Haifa and sent either to detention camps in Cypress or back to Europe. In some cases, they died at sea.

Haifa has dedicated an interesting museum to the victims
and to those who managed to break through the British
blockade. Other tourist attractions include the **Cave of
Elijah**, called the Cave of the Madonna by Christians who
hold that there the Holy Family found shelter on its return
from Egypt. Haifa is also the spiritual world center of the
Bahai faith, founded in Persia (Iran) in the early 19th
century. Followers accept teachings from many different
faiths and refuse any form of ritual or regular clergy. The
gold-domed **Bahai Shrine** with its exquisite gardens is
one of Haifa's most famous landmarks.
Haifa is also the home of Technian Institute, the well-
known research center for science and technology.

On these pages: a watch tower, stones engraved with the cross and the triangle, an evocative view of the ramparts on the sea, the crypt of the Crusader citadel, and the fleur-de-lis of France incised on a stone in the crypt.

AKKO (ACRE)

The story of Akko, like that of most of the cities in the fertile crescent, goes far back in time. The first written evidence testifying to the existence of the city dates to almost 4,000 years ago, for its name appears in the Tel el Amarna tablets dated around the 14th century B.C. Throughout its long history, many conquering peoples have laid claim to this hospitable port. It thus became Aka of the Greeks, Ptolemais of Ptolemy II Philadelphus, Colonia Claudia Felix of Emperor Claudius, Saint Jean d'Acre of the Crusaders and Akka of the Arabs. In 1948, with the end of the British Mandate and the entry of the Hagannah (Jewish self-defence organization at the time of the Mandate), the city once more took its ancient biblical name (Judges 1:31).

The characteristic fishing port and the walls of the citadel which dominate the sea.

Occupied by the Egyptians in the 15th century B. C., it was not conquered by the tribes of Israel until a late date. This is why the Hebrews always considered it to be outside the boundaries of the Land of Israel. During the reign of Ptolemy Philadelphus, Akko became a very active trading and fishing port, as well as an important glass manufacturing center. Its glass factories became so famous that Pliny maintained the material had been invented there. The Romans who conquered Akko in 48 B.C. made it a major stopover on the first paved road they built through Israel, reactivating the old route of the Via Maris which had been made unusable by Alexander's armies. From 636 to 1104 the city was in Arab hands. Wiped out by the Genovese fleet during the First Crusade, it was retaken by Saladin in 1187 and finally conquered by the legendary Richard the Lion-Hearted in 1191. After the fall of Jerusalem in 1192, Akko was called Saint Jean d'Acre after the Knights of Saint John who, together with the Templars and the Teutonic Knights, were garrisoned there. It became the capital of the Latin Kingdom of the East and the seat of many trading companies from Venice, Genoa, Amalfi and Marseilles. This period of prosperity came to an end in

The Khan el-Umdan Caravanserai and a typical street in the souk.

1291 when the Mamelukes sacked and razed the city to the ground, after which it was abandoned for about 450 years. Under the bloody rule of Ahmed Jezzar the city entered a new era of splendor. In the second half of the 18th century, this Bosnian adventurer consolidated a vast kingdom whose lands extended from Tripoli to Damascus. His cruelty has become proverbial but he was also an inspired town planner. He completely renovated Akko, not hesitating to plunder neighboring Roman-Byzantine palaces and ruins in his efforts to make the city more beautiful. When visiting Akko's mosques, baths or caravansaries, therefore, it is not unusual to find capitals, friezes or columns from ancient buildings. To keep Napoleon's army at bay, Ahmed Jezzar had the city enclosed in a second circle of walls. During the 19th century, Akko figured prominently in the alliance between the Turkish empire and the British crown. The city declined, its port silted up, and the ancient capital of so many ephimeral kingdoms fell to the rank of prison fortress. In 1948, the forces of the Hagannah took possession of the city which thus came under Israeli administration.

Signs of Akko's rich history are everywhere. The

Mosque of al-Jazzar, the largest in Akko, was built on the vaulted rooms of the Crusader fortress and elaborately decorated with arabesques and marble. The Turkish baths have now been converted into a museum. The once sumptuous caravansaries (khans) used to shelter camel caravans which stopped at Akko. These imposing structures attest to the commercial importance of the city until the mid-19th century, when merchants in precious stones from Venice, Marseilles, Amsterdam, Antwerp and London came here to buy their wares directly. Undoubtedly, the visitor to Akko will be most impressed by the **Crusader citadel**, a large subterranean fortress which was the administrative headquarters of the Crusader religious orders from 1191 to 1291. It is one of the most interesting and oldest examples of medieval Gothic architecture. In the times of Richard the Lion-Hearted and Louis IX, religious functions and councils of war took place in the vast hall, commonly called the **Crypt**, which probably also served as a refectory for the Crusaders. Some of the brackets in the room are sculptured with the fleur-de-lis of France, the first time that this motif appears in European heraldry. Actually this symbol, adopted by many Catholic sovereigns, seems to have been borrowed from Islamic heraldry, for the iris is the emblem of none other than the «ferocious» Saladin.

A street in the market; three views of the lovely Mosque of al-Jazzar and so-called «Grand Meneir» of the Crusader citadel.

Panorama of Nazareth, dominated by the Basilica of the Annunciation, of which a view of the imposing side and the interior of the crypt with the grotto of the Annunciation are also shown.

NAZARETH

In Arabic and in Hebrew, Nazareth means «guardian,» perhaps referring to the town's strategic location above the Valley of Esdraelon. Later, the allusion was made to Nazareth's role as guardian of Christian tradition for there the Franciscan fathers nurture and preserve the spiritual heritage of the town.

Although the area had been settled as far back as the Middle Bronze Age, the town where the child Jesus lived was never particularly important as a city. On the contrary, it was despised and its inhabitants were contemptuously called «notzrim» («Christians»). It was subject to attacks by the Romans and later by its aggressive Arab neighbors. In 1099, with the arrival of the Crusaders, Nazareth became a bishopric and the administrative center of the Galilee. It was repeatedly conquered and lost by the Christian warriors, destroyed finally by the

Mamelukes in 1263 and subsequently abandoned. Not until the Franciscans returned in the 17th century did Christians resettle the town.

The population of modern Nazareth is extremely varied. Moslem Arabs and Jews make up two-thirds of the town's inhabitants while the last third is comprised of Christian Arabs, Catholic Greeks of the Melchite rite, Greek Orthodox, Roman Catholics, Maronite Christians and other smaller groups, all of whom have their places of worship.

The largest church in the city is the **Basilica of the Annunciation**, erected over the grotto where, according to tradition, the Archangel Gabriel announced to Mary that she would be the mother of Christ. This is the fifth building constructed on the sacred site. The first church built here in 356 A.D. was that of Helena, mother of

◄ *The upper church, with the large mosaic in the center representing the Triumph of the Universal Church.*

◄ *The Church of St. Joseph, built on the spot where Joseph's carpentry shop supposedly was.*

The market of Nazareth.

The so-called Well of the Virgin, where Mary is said to have gone to draw water and where she met the Archangel who greeted her with the words «Ave Maria». The Church of St. Gabriel has been built over the site.

Emperor Constantine, the first royal champion of Christianity. Other churches were built by the Byzantines, the Crusaders and finally the Franciscans, whose sanctuary was pulled down in 1955 to make room for the present basilica completed in 1969. On the lower level of the church is the «Grotto of the Annunciation» where the words «Ave Maria» are carved on a column marking the place where the Archangel is said to have appeared.

The **Church of Saint Joseph** also belongs to the Franciscans and is built above older structures, one of which is believed to have been Joseph's carpentry shop. The honor is contested by the Convent of the Ladies of Nazareth and that of Saint Gabriel who both claim to be located at the saint's workshop. This is not the only ecclesiastical dispute in Nazareth. According to the Greek Orthodox **Church of St. Gabriel**, the angel appeared to Mary near the **Well of the Virgin**, whose waters originate in the spring right under the church. Other religious buildings which merit a visit are the Salesian Church, considered to be a masterpiece of 20th-century architecture, the Coptic Church, the Maronite Church, the chapel known as Mensa Christi, and the White Mosque. The latter stands on the remains of the synagogue where Christ was attacked by a crowd of his fellow citizens who tried to throw him over a cliff (Luke 4:14-31). The Church of the Madonna of Fear is in the place where it is said that Mary, when she learned of the attempt on her son's life, became greatly afraid.

◄ *Mount Tabor which dominates the plain of Esdraelon.*

A thriving banana plantation on the banks of the sea of Galilee.

◄ *Exterior and interior of the Church of the Transfiguration and the excavations of the original church.*

MOUNT TABOR

Mount Tabor looms up gently over the Jezreel Valley in a region where every stone seems imbued with a historical and religious past. The name in Arabic, Jebel Tor, mountain of the bull, recalls an ancient Phoenician cult and hints at the mount's early, albeit pagan, sacred character. The name of Tabor appears frequently in the Bible: the mountain marked the ancient boundaries between the tribal territories of Zebulun, Issachar and Naphtali (Joshua 19:10, 17, 32); on it the prophetess Deborah ordered Barak to call together ten thousand warriors and declare war against the army of Jabin, king of Canaan, who had oppressed the children of Israel for twenty years (Judges 4:1-16). The prophet Hosea mentions it when he reproves the Israelite chiefs for their idolatrous corruption (Hosea 5:1). Lastly, it is on Tabor that according to tradition the miracle of the transfiguration of Christ took place (Matthew 17:1-5; Luke 9:28-35). In remembrance of this, the **Church of the Transfiguration** was built here in 1923, the last of a series of religious buildings that were destroyed in past centuries, usually as a result of war.

SEA OF GALILEE AND TIBERIAS

The Sea of Galilee and the city of Tiberias located on its western shore, lie within the Great Syrian-African Rift Valley. The temperate climate, natural beauty and presence of therapeutic thermal springs have made this place a favorite health and holiday resort. The waters of the lake, extremely rich in fish, have a maximum depth of 49 meters and provide most of the country's fresh water supply. There is normally a pleasant breeze during the hot season, but late in the afternoons, sudden violent storms sometimes occur. This immediately recalls the Gospel passage in which Jesus calms the agitated waters of the lake. «And behold, there arose a great tempest in the sea, insomuch that the ship was covered with the waves but he was asleep. And his disciples came to him and awoke him saying, Lord, save us we perish. And he saith unto them, Why are ye fearful, O ye of little faith? Then he arose, and rebuked the winds and the sea, and there was a great calm.» (Matthew 8:23-26). The shores of the lake provided a serene setting for Christ's teachings. The Gospels

◄ *View of Tiberias.*

◄ *Yardenit, where the Jordan River leaves the Sea of Galilee is the site where tradition claims that Jesus was baptized by John. Many pilgrims visit this holy site to be baptized.*

Two views of the excavations in the city of Hammat: the mosaics in the synagogue are particularly fine.

recount many episodes as having occured here, including the meeting of James, John and Simon, the miraculous Draft of Fish, the Multiplication of the Loaves and the Walking on the Waters.

In 18 A. D., Herod Antipas founded the city of Tiberias, destined to become one of the most important centers of Jewish learning and culture after the destruction of the Temple. The Jerusalem Talmud was largely completed here in the 4th century and vowel symbols were added to the Hebrew alphabet. After having been destroyed more than once by earthquake, the modern city was rebuilt two kilometers north of the remains of Roman Tiberias, where the thermal springs and spas are today.

The remains of the old synagogue.

CAPERNAUM

Capernaum, where Christ went to live after he left Nazareth, is located on the northern shore of the Sea of Galilee near the ancient Via Maris route to Syria. The Gospels contain many passages about Jesus' teaching and miracles in Capernaum, although he chastised the inhabitants for their lack of belief and repentence: «And thou, Capernaum, which art exalted until heaven, shalt be brought down to hell, for if the mighty works which have been done in thee had been done in Sodom, it would have remained until this day» (Matthew 11:23). Evidence of the ancient town's splendor can be seen in the ancient **synagogue**, one of the earliest and best preserved of the Galilean synagogues. It is not, however, the one where Jesus first taught his disciples (Mark 1:21) nor the one built by the centurion whose servant was miraculously healed (Luke 7:5). It dates from the fourth century, probably from the time of Emperor Julian, when the imperial goverment gave the Jewish community permission to reconstruct the original synagogue there. The hypothesis of imperial financing seems confirmed by the presence of ornamental motifs such as eagles, lions, griffins, dates, acanthus, shells, etc.

TABGHA

The name is an Arabic mispronunciation of the original Greek «Heptapegon», meaning «Seven Springs.» Five springs are still discernible but they are salty. This explains why they never attracted large-scale settlement. One tradition has it that Job was healed of his ills in these therapeutic springs. But Tabgha is more famous in Christian tradition as the site of the Multiplication of Loaves and Fishes. In memory of this extraordinary event, a basilica was built here in the 4th century, superceded by another in the 5th century, and it is still possible to admire parts of their splendid **mosaic floors** enclosed in the new church of Tabgha. Animals and plants are represented with an incredibly refined sense of color and execution. In Tabgha the Benedictine order founded a monastery next to which is the Franciscan church of the Primacy of St. Peter, where Christ is said to have reappeared to his disciples for the third time after the resurrection.

The Sanctuary built on the Mount of the Beatitudes.

Two details of the mosaic pavement in the Church of the Multiplication of the Loaves in Tabgha.

The synagogue of Rabbi Isaac Luria and that of Isaac Aboab.

A characteristic corner of the artists' quarter.

Two views of Safed, with its picturesque artistic ► disorder.

SAFED

Safed lies on the western slope of Mount Canaan and is the highest city in Israel. It is known as the city of Jewish mysticism. When the Jews were expelled from Spain in 1492, Safed, at the time under a tolerant Moslem rule, offered refuge to many, including men of great talent and intellect. Among them were Isaac Luria, Haim Vital, Moshe Cordovero, Israel Najara, and Joseph Caro who dedicated themselves to the study of the holy texts, particularly the Pentateuch. They studied and developed the «kabalah», an attempt to unlock the secret, mystical truths contained in the scriptures.

Today the city is divided into well-defined districts, including the **citadel** (Hametsuda), the **quarter of the old synagogues**, the **artists' quarter** and the suburb of Canaan, each of which offers picturesque walks through a hilly maze of narrow streets.

107

Various views of the Kibbutz Ayelet Hashahar, whose name means «morning star».

KIBBUTZ AYELET HASHAHAR

In 1918 Kibbutz Ayelet Hashahar was founded near the archaeological site of Tel Hazor. The kibbutz maintains a museum in which are housed fascinating artifacts gathered from the tel, the most powerful city in the area at the time of Joshua's entry into Canaan. Vases, jewelery, spearheads and basalt statuettes were found during excavation of the site which began in 1928. The digs brought to light a lower city and an acropolis connected by a tunnel 38 meters deep, numerous princely tombs, a palace, a great temple with numerous cult objects and the tomb of the king of Hazor named in the Book of Joshua (11:10) and in the Book of Judges (4:2).

◀ *The snow-topped Mount Hermon and the remains of the Crusader fortress of Nimrod, 13th century.*

Cultivations in the Golan heights.

Monument erected to the national hero Joseph Trumpeldor.

GOLAN

Bordered on the west by the Sea of Galilee and the River Jordan, on the north by **Mount Hermon**, on the east and on the south by the Raqqad and Yarmuk Rivers, the Golan Heights mark the extreme northern boundary of the State of Israel. Once famous for its fertility – the Golan is the historical Bash'an of the Bible – it is now cultivated by over twenty Jewish settlements founded since the 1967 Six Day War when Israel conquered the area. Once the Syrian military withdrew from the Golan, only a few groups of Druse and Circassian farmers remained. Their communities can be seen there today.

The Golan is dominated by Mount Hermon whose slopes are often white with snow. In Israeli territory, it rises to 2,224 meters. It is a favorite winter sport resort since snow often lasts from November to March.

The River Jordan springs from the slopes of Mount Hermon, fed by the melting winter snows. It flows downward to the Sea of Galilee, 210 meters below sea level.

Two characteristic Druse figures.

Vestiges of the ancient temple dedicated to Pan, in Banyas.

One of the three springs of the Jordan, fed by the ►
waters of the river Dan: the name Jordan in fact is a
contraction of the Hebrew Yored Dan, which means
«coming from Dan».

BANYAS

Covered with green woods and the gurgling song of streams and waterfalls, Banyas is a natural sanctuary tucked into the slopes of Mount Hermon. The Canaanites who first lived here worshipped a water god, while the Greeks dedicated the area to the cult of Pan, a god of nature. The niches of the temple they built for him can still be seen near the main spring. «Banyas» is apparently the Arabic mispronunciation of the ancient Greek name, Paneas. In Roman times, the town was known as Caesarea Philippi, mentioned in the Gospels (Matthew 16:13; Mark 8:27). Destroyed by an earthquake, Banyas was then occupied by the Crusaders who took over the nearby fortress of Subeiba (Nimrod's Castle) in 1130. The mountain-top fortress was built, according to local legend, by the king of Babel, son of Cam «the first to hold power above the earth.» When the Crusaders left, it fell into the hands of the secret sect called the «Hashshashin,» whose members were addicted to hashish and were often involved in political murders. Their very name became a symbol of violence, the origin of the word assassin. The imposing remains of the castle can still be seen today, silent witness to its mysterious and fascinating past.

On these pages, various views of the Bedouin market of Beersheba.

BEERSHEBA

Capital of the arid region of the Negev, the city of Beersheba is a modern city built at the edge of the desert on a site rich in history and biblical references. Considered by archaeologists to be one of the oldest human settlements in the country, Beersheba was often mentioned in the Hebrew scriptures and from them receives its name. Beersheba means «the well of the oath» in remembrance of the well dug by Abraham, where the Patriarch and the King of Gerar, Abimelech, swore never to do each other harm (Gen. 21:23-23). The prophet Elijah sojourned in this region; Isaac, Jacob and Joshua passed through the area; the people of Israel settled here after their return form Babylonia and Egypt. In the centuries that followed, Beersheba was nothing but a modest village at the gates of the desert. It became somewhat more important only at the end of the 19th century when the Turkish authorities attempted to transform it into an administrative center that controlled the southern territories of Palestine.

After the English conquest of 1917, however, the small urban settlement seemed forgotten until the 1948 Independence War, when it became the object of contention between Egyptians and Israelis. Israel finally managed to hold the region. Since then, Beersheba has developed so rapidly that today it can be considered one of the most

The arid plain on which Beersheba is situated, with green cultivations scattered here and there, is the gateway to the Neghev desert.

The famous Ben Gurion University, with its futuristic Library.

The Museum of Beersheba is in a mosque in the ▶ old city. Shown here are some of the rooms.

vital cities in the country, complete with modern tourist infrastructures and all the services needed in a large urban center. Besides an active industrial district which provides work for inhabitants throughout the region, the present capital of the Negev can also boast numerous art centers, schools of all kinds, the prestigious **Ben Gurion University** and a well-stocked **museum** housed in the Old City's mosque. The dominant characteristic of Beersheba is undoubtedly its cosmopolitanism. It is inhabited by people from more than 70 countries, from the first immigrants who came from Morocco and Rumania to the families recently arrived in Israel from the Soviet Union and Argentina. The Bedouins, who live in a number of neighboring satellite settlements or in tents scattered throughout the area, crowd the city streets especially on Thursday morning, marketing day, one of the principal tourist attractions of the city. Fine carpets, cushions, camel saddles, typical Arab headdresses, finely worked furnishings and many other examples of Bedouin handicrafts can be bought there.

The remains of the ancient city of Mamshit are to be seen only a few kilometers from Dimona.

Following pages: two views of the desert zone of the Neghev and the characteristic faces of some of its inhabitants.

DIMONA

Along the road that connects Beersheba and Sodom lies Dimona, founded in 1955 in the middle of the desert to house the workers from the various factories on the Dead Sea and the phosphate mines of Oron. Together with Yeroham, this ever-growing city constitutes the industrial heart of the Negev region. Famous for its glass factories and textile industries, Dimona was also the center of an astonishing agricultural experiment. Olives and fruit trees have been successfully planted in the desert around Dimona. A governmental project has been initiated near the town to study and extract radioactive minerals from the region and to produce heavy water.

Not far from the town, which is predominantly of French-speaking, North African origin, are the ruins of ancient **Mamshit**. This Nabatean settlement dates to the first century A. D. and archaeologists have uncovered the remains of two splendid Byzantine churches as well as the impressive hydraulic works from the Nabatean period which are still remarkably well preserved.

AVDAT

The majestic ruins of Avdat perch atop a hill that dominates the solitary scorching desert plain. Avdat was an ancient Nabatean city dating to the third century B. C. which, together with Mamshit, Haluza, Shivta and Nizzana, comprised the Nabatean Pentapolis. The Nabateans considered themselves descendants of Nabath, son of Ishmael, whose parents were Abraham and his concubine, Hagar. Nabatean culture reached its zenith between the first century B. C. and the early first century A. D. Their wealth was considerable for they controlled the caravan routes leading from the Persian Gulf and Yemen to Damascus and Gaza. Avdat was situated on the route that joined Petra, the Nabatean capital, with Eilat and Gaza. It was a prosperous trade center until the Roman Trajan conquered the Negev in 106 A. D. Excavations begun in 1952 have revealed, among other things, two churches and a bath from the Byzantine period. It seems a mystery that ancient Avdat, surrounded by desert, was a productive agricultural settlement. The Nabateans were, it appears, masters in the art of «harvesting water» as it fell on the impermeable surface of the surrounding hills. Their ancient skill is now being imitated by modern settlers in the region.

Right after the mountains, Eilat is mirrored in the blue
waters of the gulf.

Following pages: the famous submarine observatory, of
Eilat, the equally famous aquarium and a view of the
hotel complexes.

◄ The remains of the ancient Nabataean settlement
of Avdat.

EILAT

At the southernmost tip of Israel, Eilat is the country's
gateway to the Red Sea. It is located on the site of the
ancient port, Ezion-Geber, and has been fought over by
peoples in the region who hoped to ensure their access to
the Red Sea. According to tradition, this is where King
Solomon charged Hiram, king of Tyre, with building him
a fleet (I Kings 9:26-28). Modern Eilat, with an eye to the
future, does not seem to preserve any trace of its military
history. It is an attractive seaside resort which promotes
tourism and business. The port is of supreme importance
because it is Israel's only route to the Indian and Pacific
Oceans. Here, tons of merchandise are loaded and un-
loaded every day. The increasing commercial importance
of the city has stimulated rapid development and immigration, the creation of new industries and the implemen-
tation of imposing projects such as the desalination of sea
water. The ultimate aim is to reinforce communication
routes and transform this maritime center into a modern
laguna city. The lone outpost of Eilat prior to 1949 has
already become a tourist paradise of international fame.
The sun always shines, reflected by a crystal sea full of
flamboyantly colored fish and corals. These can be ad-
mired through the enormous portholes of the
Underwater Observatory.

A natural arch in the valley of Timna and the so-called «pilasters of King Solomon».

Along the road that leads to Eilat lies **Timna,** which was a mining center of considerable importance, where Israeli workmen extracted copper and manganese from the subsoil. According to tradition, this is the site of King Solomon's fabulous mines where multitudes of slaves mined and smelted copper. Archaeological excavations carried out between 1949 and 1969 under the direction of Benno Rothenberg testify to the antiquity of Timna where the ductile metal was extracted as long as 6,000 years ago.

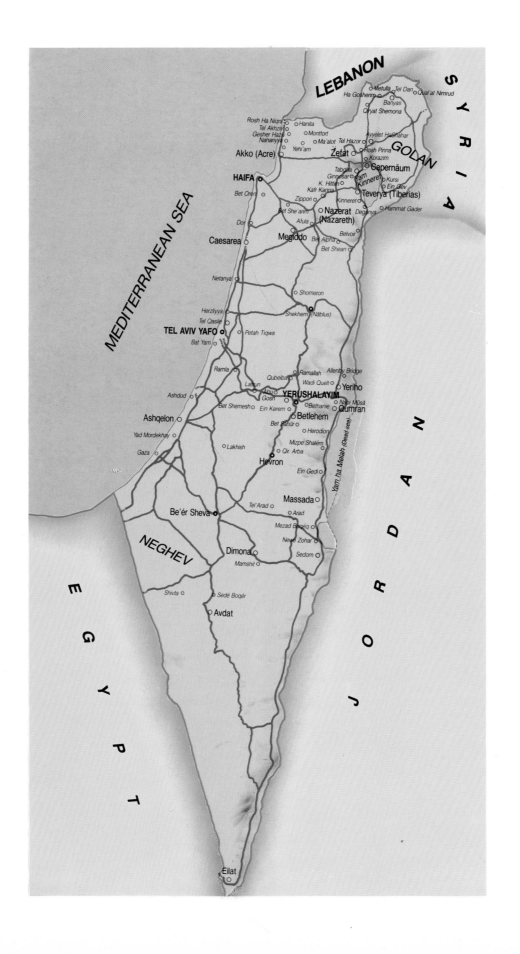